NATURAL WONDERS

Mount Kilimanjaro

The Rooftop of Africa

Galadriel Watson

W

WEIGL PUBLISHERS INC.

Published by Weigl Publishers Inc.
350 5th Avenue, Suite 3304, PMB 6G
New York, NY 10118-0069

Website: www.weigl.com

Library of Congress Cataloging-in-Publication Data

Watson, Galadriel Findlay.
 Mount Kilimanjaro/Galadriel Findlay.
        p. cm. –(Natural wonders)
 Includes index.
 ISBN: 978-1-59036-934-0 (hard cover: alk. Paper) – ISBN: 978-1-59036-1-935-7 (soft cover: alk. Paper) 1. Kilimanjaro, Mount (Tarzania)—Juvenile literature. 2. Kilimanjaro, Mount, Region (Tarzania)—Juvenile literature. I. title.
 DT449.K4W38 2009
 916.78'26—dc22

 2008016692

Printed in the United States of America

1 2 3 4 5 6 7 8 9 0 12 11 10 09 08

Project Coordinators
Heather Kissock
and Heather C. Hudak

Design
Terry Paulhus

Photograph Credits

Weigl acknowledges Getty Images as its primary image supplier.

Rebecca Marksamer: page 18, Rowan Griffiths: page 15.

Every reasonable effort has been made to trace ownership and to obtain permission to reprint copyright material. The publishers would be pleased to have any errors or omissions brought to their attention so that they may be corrected in subsequent printings.

Contents

The Pride of Tanzania

Rising high above the plains of Tanzania, Mount Kilimanjaro is the tallest mountain in Africa. Mount Kilimanjaro stands alone. It is not part of a mountain chain and is not connected to any other mountain. It is the tallest free-standing mountain in the world.

Mount Kilimanjaro ranks as one of the biggest volcanoes on Earth, although it is actually made up of three volcanoes. The tallest is a cone-shaped volcano named Kibo. Its highest peak rises 19,341 feet (5,895 meters) above sea level. Mawenzi is shorter and has a jagged peak. Shira collapsed long ago and has eroded, or worn away, so much that its once jagged peak has become a flat **plateau**.

■ **Mount Kilimanjaro has snow and ice year-round, a rare sight in Africa.**

Mount Kilimanjaro Facts

- While Mawenzi and Shira are **extinct**, Kibo is dormant. This means, it is not erupting right now, but could erupt at any time.

- Mount Kilimanjaro rises nearly 3 miles (5 kilometers) above the surrounding plains.

- Mount Kilimanjaro can be seen from a distance of more than 120 miles (190 km).

- The three volcanoes that make up Mount Kilimanjaro cover an area about 40 miles (60 km) long and 50 miles (80 km) wide.

- The highest point on Mount Kilimanjaro is Uhuru Peak. It is located on Kibo.

Mount Kilimanjaro Locator

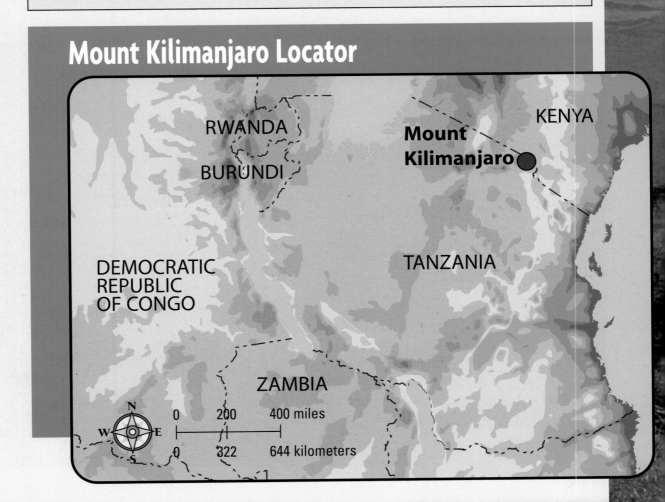

Where in the World?

Tanzania is the largest country in eastern Africa. It became a country in 1964, when the countries of Tanganyika and Zanzibar merged. Tanzania is home to more than 39 million people. It is one of the poorest countries in Africa and the world.

Mount Kilimanjaro sits in the northeastern part of Tanzania, bordering on Kenya. The mountain is about 170 miles (270 km) west of the Indian Ocean and 220 miles (350 km) south of the **equator**. The Great Rift Valley lies about 100 miles (160 km) to its west. The forces that created this valley played a key role in Mount Kilimanjaro's creation.

▬ **Remains and stone tools of the earliest known humans have been found in the Great Rift Valley.**

Puzzler

Q Mount Kilimanjaro is the highest mountain on the continent of Africa. The highest mountains for all of the continents are listed below. Using an atlas or the Internet, match the mountain to the correct continent.

1. North America
2. South America
3. Europe
4. Antarctica
5. Asia
6. Australia
7. Africa

A. Mount Elbrus
B. Vinson Massif
C. Mount Kilimanjaro
D. Mount Kosciuszko
E. Mount Aconcagua
F. Mount McKinley/Denali
G. Mount Everest

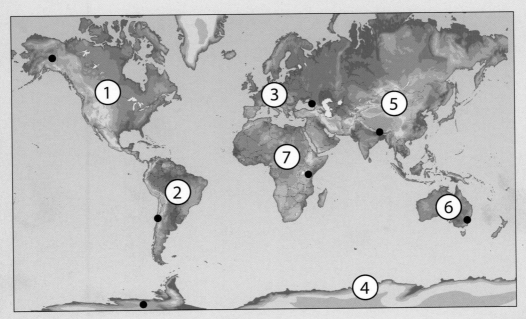

 1.F 2.E 3.A 4.B 5.G 6.D 7.C

A Trip Back in Time

Mount Kilimanjaro began forming more than 750,000 years ago. The mountain was created as a result of volcanic activity that started deep underground and broke through to the surface.

The mountain-building process did not happen overnight. It took more than 250,000 years for Mount Kilimanjaro to form. Shira was the first volcano to emerge. Mawenzi was next. Finally, about 460,000 years ago, Kibo came to be. The **lava** that flowed from Kibo attached all three volcanoes together, making the mountain that stands today.

Over time, the shape of the mountain became more defined. During the course of several **ice ages**, huge sheets of ice called glaciers cut through the rock, carving it into smooth valleys and sharp ridges.

▬ **Mawenzi's rock walls are made from lava and ashes.**

How a Volcano Forms

A thin layer of rock, called the crust, covers Earth. Beneath the crust lies a layer of melted rock called magma. The crust is broken into several pieces, called tectonic plates. These plates float around on the layer of magma. Sometimes, they bump into each other or pull apart. This movement can wear away parts of the crust, creating cracks and thin spots. Magma can burst through these weak spots. When this happens, land is pushed up, and the magma, called lava when it is above ground, spills out. This creates a volcano.

Mount Kilimanjaro was formed because of activity in the nearby Great Rift Valley, a place where two plates are pulling apart. Lava burst through the **fault** that makes up the valley. The force of the lava pushed part of Earth's crust upwards, creating the first of Kilimanjaro's three volcanoes, Shira. Similar activity later created the other two volcanoes.

▬ **Lava flows are very hot. They burn any plant and animal life they contact.**

Mount Kilimanjaro's Plants

Due to its massive size, Mount Kilimanjaro is home to five **vegetation** zones. Each zone occurs at a different **altitude** and has unique features.

The first zone is found on the lower slopes of Kilimanjaro, between 2,300 and 5,900 feet (700 and 1,800 m). At one time, the land in this zone was made up of forest and scrub. Today, the rich soils make it perfect for farming. Wildflowers are common in this zone.

At 5,900 to 9,200 feet (1,800 to 2,800 m), the second zone is a humid rain forest. Here, there is an abundance of plant life. Moss drapes the huge fig, juniper, date palm, and olive trees.

The third zone occurs at 9,200 to 13,120 feet (2,800 to 4,000 m). Vegetation such as **heath**, grasses, giant groundsels and lobelias, and wildflowers cover the slopes in this zone.

Few plants can stand the cold, dry conditions at 13,120 to 16,400 feet (4,000 to 5,000 m). The fourth zone is a hot, dry desert during the day, but the ground freezes at night. Only everlastings, mosses, **lichens**, and three types of grasses are able to survive here.

Above 16,400 feet (5,000 m), there is even less life. The fifth zone, or summit area, is home only to rocks, snow, and a few lichens.

▬ As the altitude increases, the mountain air becomes drier and colder and supports a smaller variety of life.

Giant Plants

To survive the cold, dry climate at the top of a mountain, most plants remain small. By being small, they need less water and sunlight than larger plants do. However, on Mount Kilimanjaro, some plants grow to be very large, even as the altitude increases.

On the mountain, lobelias and groundsels can grow to be as tall as a giraffe. The scorching temperatures of an African day help these plants survive at higher altitudes. However, at night, temperatures are freezing. To keep warm, both types of plants absorb heat from the Sun and store it in a unique way.

The groundsel does not shed dead leaves. Instead, the leaves remain on the plant's trunk as a form of **insulation**. The lobelia has tough outer leaves that close around the inner leaves and buds. They release a slimy substance that helps keep the plant from freezing.

■ **Most plants rely on moisture from the ground. Groundsels use their giant leaves to collect moisture from the air. This helps them survive the dry climate of the higher mountain elevations.**

Life on Mount Kilimanjaro

Mount Kilimanjaro is home to many animals, including 140 types of mammals. Each vegetation zone has unique features that support different creatures. While some zones have a large variety of wildlife, others are inhabited by only the smallest life forms.

In the lush rain forest of the second zone, the trees are alive with monkeys and birds. Large animals, including elephants, lions, leopards, and giraffes, travel through the jungle growth. African hunting dogs and birds of prey, such as buzzards, eagles, and bearded vultures, live here as well.

The extreme altitude keeps many animals from living higher up the mountain. Lions, wild dogs, and elands have been found living in the third zone. Even fewer animals dwell in the fourth zone. These include birds, rodents, and insects. Animals are unable to survive the harsh climates of the fifth zone.

■ A type of monkey called the Abyssian black-and-white colobus lives in the forests of Mount Kilimanjaro National Park.

Elands

Elands are some of the many mammals that live on Mount Kilimanjaro. These large animals look similar to cows and can grow to be about 6.6 feet (2 m) high at the shoulders. They weigh between 600 and 2,200 pounds (272 and 1,000 kilograms).

Male and female elands have long, twisting horns that grow from the top of their head. As they age, eland fur turns from tan to gray to black.

In addition to Kilimanjaro, elands can be found living in the grasslands of central and southern Africa. Here, they graze on plant matter, such as twigs, branches, grasses, and leaves.

Elands are the largest members of the antelope family.

Early Explorers

Johannes Rebmann, a German **missionary**, arrived in East Africa in 1846. Rebmann traveled the countryside to teach Africans about **Christianity**. On May 11, 1848, he became the first European to see Mount Kilimanjaro.

Rebmann reported his find back to Europe. However, few people believed he had found a snow-covered mountain in Africa, so close to the equator. Support for Rebmann's claims came 12 years later. German explorer Baron Karl Klaus von der Decken and British geologist Richard Thornton surveyed the mountain. They were the first Europeans to see Mount Kilimanjaro since Rebmann had visited the site 13 years earlier.

Decken and Thornton attempted to climb the mountain, but bad weather stopped them from climbing very high. In 1862, Decken and explorer Otto Kersten made another attempt to climb Mount Kilimanjaro, but poor weather stopped their team at about 14,000 feet (4,267 m). Seventeen years passed before the first Europeans, Hans Meyer and Ludwig Purtscheller, reached the top of the mountain.

Thousands of climbers attempt to reach Kibo's summit each year.

Biography

Hans Meyer (1858–1929)

As a child, Hans Meyer enjoyed learning about geography. His family published books, and Meyer often read about faraway places. At age 23, he left home and traveled around the world for two years. Meyer then worked as a professor of geography at Germany's Leipzig University.

In 1887, Meyer made his first attempt to climb Mount Kilimanjaro. He was poorly equipped and had to turn back. Meyer tried again the next year, but a war in the area kept him from completing the trek. The following year, Meyer returned with Austrian climber Ludwig Purtscheller. On October 6, 1889, Meyer and Purtscheller became the first Europeans to reach the highest peak, Kibo's summit. Meyer planted a German flag on the summit.

Facts of Life

Born: March 22, 1858

Hometown: Hildburghausen, Germany

Occupation: Geography professor

Died: July 15, 1929

The Big Picture

Volcanoes can be found on all of Earth's continents. As a group, the highest volcanoes on each continent are known as the seven volcanic summits. This map shows where each of these volcanoes is located.

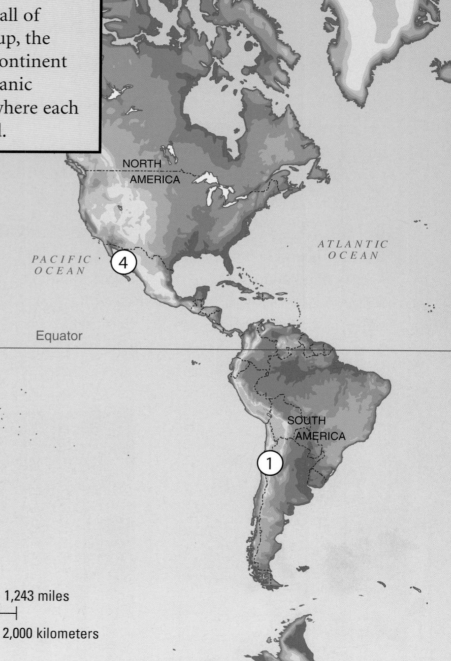

NORTH AMERICA

PACIFIC OCEAN

ATLANTIC OCEAN

④

Equator

SOUTH AMERICA

①

⑦

0	623	1,243 miles
0	1,000	2,000 kilometers

Map Legend

	Volcanic Summit	Continent	Elevation (ft)	Elevation (m)
1.	Ojos del Salado	South America	22,572	6,880
2.	Kilimanjaro	Africa	19,340	5,895
3.	Elbrus	Europe	18,510	5,642
4.	Pico de Orizaba	North America	18,491	5,636
5.	Damavand	Asia	18,406	5,610
6.	Mount Giluwe	Australia/Oceania	14,331	4,368
7.	Mount Sidley	Antarctica	14,058	4,285

Living on Mount Kilimanjaro

Archaeologists have found stone bowls at the base of Mount Kilimanjaro. These show that people have lived near the mountain for at least 3,000 years. Today, the area is inhabited mostly by a group of people called the Chagga.

The Chagga have lived in the area around Mount Kilimanjaro for about 400 years. One of Tanzania's largest cultural groups, the Chagga reside on the lower levels of the mountain. They use the land for farming, taking advantage of the rich soils and plentiful water that runs from the mountain's glaciers. Important crops include coffee and bananas, as well as barley, wheat, and sugar. The Chagga raise cattle, and some people collect honey.

Some Chagga still practice the traditional ways of their ancestors. Many groups have adopted European beliefs and ways of life. They value education and work in fields such as medicine and law. In most cases, the guides and porters that travel with tourists as they climb Kilimanjaro are Chagga.

Chagga markets sell produce and other goods.

Language Essentials

Most of the people in Tanzania speak a language called Swahili. The Chagga people that live around Mount Kilimanjaro also speak Kichagga. With a friend, try practicing the Swahili words below.

English	Kichagga
Hello	Jambo
Good bye	Kwaheri
No problem	Hakuna matata
Thank you	Asante
How are you?	Habari?
Very well	Mzuri sana

Legends from Mount Kilimanjaro

When Johannes Rebmann first saw Mount Kilimanjaro, the local people told him its summit was covered with a strange white powder that looked like silver. They believed that evil spirits protected the mountain's treasures, and they would punish any person who tried to climb the mountain. Rebmann soon learned that the silver was snow and that the evil spirits were the extreme cold. Both the snow and the cold could easily hurt a person who was not dressed for the weather.

The Chagga people still have great respect for the mountain. To them, it is the home of the gods. Traditionally, the Chagga would bury their dead so that the body was facing Mount Kilimanjaro. They may have believed that the summit led to the **afterlife**.

▬ Some people believe it is good luck for a person descending from Kilimanjaro's summit to say "hello" to climbers who are still making their way to the top.

Jagged Mawenzi

Mawenzi is known for its jagged peak. Scientists say that this peak formed as a result of erosion. The Chagga have a different story. They believe that the volcanoes were brothers who had a fight.

Mawenzi once looked like Kibo. One day, Mawenzi's fire died, so he asked Kibo for help. Kibo gave Mawenzi coal. Mawenzi decided this was a good way to get fire. Day after day, Mawenzi let his fire die. Each day, Kibo gave Mawenzi coal. However, Mawenzi never thanked Kibo for his generosity.

One day, Mawenzi saw that Kibo was not home. He decided to help himself to all of Kibo's coal. When Kibo returned and saw what Mawenzi had done, he was very mad. Kibo hit Mawenzi on the head, giving him the jagged peak he has today. Kibo had to work hard to restart his fire. This caused lava to spew from his belly.

■ **Kibo felt so bad about hurting Mawenzi and erupting that he promised never to act so violently again.**

Natural Attractions

Each year, thousands of people attempt hiking to the summit of Mount Kilimanjaro. There are many routes up the mountain. Most people take four to six days to get to the top.

The hike can be done using standard hiking equipment. However, climbing Mount Kilimanjaro is still considered to be a huge challenge. Trying to climb the mountain too quickly is dangerous. This is because oxygen levels decrease as the altitude increases. There is half the amount of oxygen at the summit as there is at sea level. Climbers must let their bodies slowly adjust to the decreasing oxygen levels. If they do not, climbers may suffer from altitude sickness, an illness that causes headaches, sleepiness, and muscle weakness that can be deadly. In addition to a lack of oxygen, climbers must cover more than 50 miles (80 km) of land without the use of vehicles.

Mount Kilimanjaro is the setting for many athletic events. The Kilimanjaro Marathon is a 26.2-mile (42.2-km) foot race around the base of the mountain. Another event, the Kiliman Adventure Challenge, includes a climb to the summit, a mountain bike race, and a marathon.

▬ People who become ill or injured on the mountain must be taken down as quickly as possible.

Mount Kilimanjaro National Park

A large part of Mount Kilimanjaro is a national park. Mount Kilimanjaro National Park was formed in 1973, and it was opened to the public in 1977. It protects wildlife, maintains trails, and provides mountain rescue teams.

The national park covers 292 square miles (755 sq km). It includes the areas above the tree line, as well as six **corridors** through the Kilimanjaro Forest Reserve. The reserve was created to keep the logging and farming industries from causing more damage to the rain forests.

In 1987, the mountain was named a United Nations Educational and Cultural Organization (UNESCO) World Heritage Site. UNESCO identifies places around the world that are important to all people. These landmarks are protected from being destroyed by tourism and neglect.

The mountain's ice fields and glacier are part of Mount Kilimanjaro National Park.

Protecting Kilimanjaro

A poor country such as Tanzania welcomes tourism, but too many tourists can harm important sites, including Mount Kilimanjaro. The trails that have been created for hiking have cut through vegetation, and people who walk off the trails damage the plant life that lives on the mountain. Hikers can contribute to soil erosion simply by walking on the ground. When camps are being set up for the night, hikers sometimes cut down trees to use as firewood. Litter in the form of plastic bags, water bottles, toilet paper, and candy wrappers is strewn on the ground.

In recent years, the park has been trying to stop these negative effects. Now, ecotourism practices are encouraged to keep the park free of clutter and preserve its natural appeal. Limits are placed on the number of people allowed into the park at one time. Trails are repaired when they become eroded, and people are no longer allowed to cut down trees. At one time, the remains of campfires and trash littered the mountain. Today, it is illegal to collect and burn plants on Kilimanjaro, and people must remove all items that they bring with them to the mountain.

■ **Of the nearly 11,000 people that enter Mount Kilimanjaro National Park each year, only 40 percent reach the summit.**

Education programs have been developed to teach people about keeping Mount Kilimanjaro clean. Visitors, porters, wardens, guides, and people who live in the community are taught ways they can help preserve the mountain environment. They learn how to keep trails clean, report **poachers**, and spot forest fires.

Should visitors be allowed to climb Mount Kilimanjaro?	
YES	NO
Visitors bring money to a very poor country.	Visitors damage the plants and soil on the mountain.
People who see the mountain firsthand will want to help protect it.	People can experience the beauty of the mountain by simply viewing it.
Most visitors know how to properly dispose of their garbage.	Visitors litter the mountain with candy wrappers, plastic bags, and water bottles.

Timeline

750,000 years ago
The first volcano, Shira, forms.

500,000 years ago
Mawenzi, the second
volcano, forms.

460,000 years ago
Kibo forms.

10,000 years ago
Temperatures start to
increase, and plants that
need cold climates to survive
retreat to mountain slopes.

1000 BC
People live around the base
of Mount Kilimanjaro.

AD 1600s
The Chagga move
to the area.

1848
Johannes Rebmann becomes
the first European to see
Mount Kilimanjaro.

Elephants are a common sight in Tanzania and on Mount Kilimanjaro.

1861
Richard Thornton, of Britain,
attempts to climb Mount
Kilimanjaro. He does not
reach the top.

1889
Germany's Dr. Hans Meyer
and Austria's Ludwig
Purtscheller become the first
Europeans to reach the peak.

At one time, Kilimanjaro's peak was known for its massive amount of snow. As temperatures rise, the snow is melting.

Mount Kilimanjaro has a glacier near its summit.

Kilimanjaro's giant lobelias grow as tall as 30 feet (9 m).

1921
The game preserve is made into a forest preserve as well.

1973
Mount Kilimanjaro National Park is formed.

1977
The park opens to the public.

1989
Mount Kilimanjaro becomes a UNESCO World Heritage Site.

1993
The park creates a management plan that helps protect the mountain and minimize the effects of tourism.

2001
Bruno Brunod of Italy becomes the fastest person to reach the summit. It takes him only 5 hours and 38 minutes.

2004
Tanzania's Simon Mtuy becomes the fastest person to summit and descend the mountain. He does this in 8 hours and 27 minutes.

Early 1900s
Part of Mount Kilimanjaro is set aside as a game preserve.

1914
Frau von Ruckteschell becomes the first woman to climb Mount Kilimanjaro.

What Have You Learned?

True or False?

Decide whether the following statements are true or false. If the statement is false, make it true.

1. Mount Kilimanjaro is made up of three volcanoes.

2. Plants and animals are similar all over the mountain.

3. Some plants survive the cold by growing really big.

4. Uhuru Peak is Mount Kilimanjaro's highest point.

5. Most people in Tanzania speak Kichagga.

ANSWERS

1. True. The volcanoes are Kibo, Mawenzi, and Shira.

2. False. There are many types of plants and animals.

3. True. Examples include lobelias and groundsels.

4. True. It is located on Kibo.

5. False. Kichagga is the language of the Chagga people, but most Tanzanians speak Swahili.

Short Answer

Answer the following questions using information from the book.

1. What are two ways visitors can harm the mountain?

2. What is the Great Rift Valley?

3. What is magma called after it erupts?

4. Do monkeys live on Mount Kilimanjaro?

5. Who was the first European to see Mount Kilimanjaro?

ANSWERS

1. They may trample on plants or leave garbage behind
2. An area in which two tectonic plates are pulling apart
3. Lava
4. Yes. They live in the rain forest.
5. Missionary Johannes Rebmann

Multiple Choice

Choose the best answer for the following questions.

1. What is the name of the people who live at the base of Mount Kilimanjaro?
   a) the Swahilians
   b) the Chagga
   c) the Kichagga
   d) the Tanzanians

2. Which volcano has a jagged peak?
   a) Kibo
   b) Shira
   c) Mawenzi
   d) none of them

3. Why is it dangerous to climb the mountain too fast?
   a) you may get tired
   b) your muscles might get sore
   c) you could catch a cold
   d) you might get altitude sickness

4. What do you call a volcano that is not erupting right now, but could erupt at any time?
   a) dormant
   b) in transition
   c) extinct
   d) active

ANSWERS

1. b
2. c
3. d
4. a

Find Out for Yourself

Books

Amin, Mohamed, Graham Mercer, and David Pluth. *Kilimanjaro: The Great White Mountain of Africa*. Nairobi: Camerapix Publishers International, 2001.

Salkeld, Audrey. *Kilimanjaro: To the Roof of Africa*. Washington: National Geographic Society, 2002.

Websites

Use the Internet to find out more about Mount Kilimanjaro and the latest expeditions to its summit.

NOVA/Volcano Above the Clouds
www.pbs.org/wgbh/nova/kilimanjaro
This site offers information about the mountain's ecosystems and climates, as well as the seven summits.

Volcano World
http://volcano.und.nodak.edu
Learn about volcanic eruptions on this site.

Mount Kilimanjaro National Park
www.tanzaniaparks.com/kili.htm
Visit this site to see photographs of the mountain.

Skill Matching Page

What did you learn? Look at the questions in the "Skills" column. Compare them to the page number of the answers in the "Page" column. Refresh your memory by reading the "Answer" column below.

SKILLS	ANSWER	PAGE
What facts did I learn from this book?	I learned that Mount Kilimanjaro is the tallest mountain in Africa.	4
What skills did I learn?	I learned how to read maps.	5, 7, 16–17
What activities did I do?	I answered the questions in the quizzes.	7, 28–29
How can I find out more?	I can read the books and visit the websites found on the Find Out for Yourself page.	30
How can I get involved?	I can protect my environment by staying on marked trails and getting rid of my garbage properly.	24–25

Glossary

afterlife: life after death

altitude: the measurement above sea level of different locations on Earth

Christianity: a religion based on the teachings of Jesus Christ

corridors: long stretches of land between two areas

equator: the imaginary line that runs east to west around the widest part of Earth, dividing it in two

extinct: no longer exists

fault: a break in Earth's crust

heath: small leathery shrubs

ice ages: periods when Earth was covered with glaciers

insulation: the act of protecting something against heat loss

lava: hot, liquid rock that flows from a volcano

lichens: a plant-like organism that is able to grow in harsh conditions

missionary: a person who introduces a religion to people in other countries

plateau: an area of land having a raised, flat surface

poachers: people who hunt illegally

vegetation: the types of plants that are found in a specific area

Index